Art of the Far North

Art of the Far North

Inuit Sculpture, Drawing, and Printmaking

BY CAROL FINLEY

LERNER PUBLICATIONS COMPANY

Lerner Publications Company
241 First Avenue North
Minneapolis, Minnesota 55401

Website address: www.lernerbooks.com

Library of Congress Cataloging-in-Publication Data

Finley, Carol.
    Art of the Far North : Inuit sculpture, drawing, and printmaking / Carol Finley.
        p.   cm. — (Art around the world)
    Includes bibliographical references and index.
    Summary: Provides a brief history of the Inuit people and discusses their customs as a background for understanding their sculpture, drawing, and printmaking.
    ISBN 0-8225-2075-3 (alk. paper)
    1. Inuit art—Juvenile literature. 2. Inuit—Material culture—Juvenile literature. 3. Inuit—Social life and customs—Juvenile literature   [1. Inuit art. 2. Inuit—Social life and customs.]
    I. Title. II. Series.
    E99.E7F517 1998
    704.03'9712—dc21   97-28375

Manufactured in the United States of America
1 2 3 4 5 6 - JR - 03 02 01 00 99 98

Contents

chapter one

The Story
of the
Inuit People

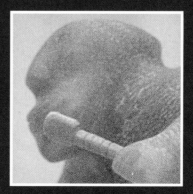

Huskies are pulling a dogsled
on sea ice.

An Inuit man paddles his kayak in front of an iceberg.

THE INUIT ARE ONE OF THE NATIVE PEOPLES of North America. They were formerly called *Eskimos,* a Native American word that means "eaters of raw meat." They prefer to be known as *Inuit,* a word that means "the people" in their language. The Inuit live in the far northern part of the continent, near the Arctic Circle.

The climatic conditions in the Arctic are among the most severe on earth. During the long winter, average temperatures range between –20°F and –30°F. Freezing winds sweep across the land at 70 miles per hour, making the region feel even colder. In the northern part of the Arctic, the ground underneath a small layer of topsoil is permanently frozen. This frozen layer is called permafrost.

Within the Arctic Circle, the days grow so short in winter that on December 22 the sun does not rise above the horizon at all. It is a day of continuous darkness. In summer, the reverse happens. On June 22, the sun never sets. It is a day of continuous sunlight. The farther north a person goes, the more days there will be of continuous darkness in winter and continuous light in summer. If a person were to stand at the North Pole—at the center of the Arctic—every direction in which he or she looked would be south.

Much of the Arctic land is above the timberline. Trees do not grow north of the timberline because of the soil conditions, the short growing season, and the severe cold. Without trees there is no supply of wood, except for the driftwood that may wash up on ocean shores. Some berries, shrubs, and lichens (mosslike growths) do grow in the Arctic, but the crops and livestock that provide the primary diet for people in most other parts of the world can't be grown there. Nevertheless, the Inuit have managed to carve out a livelihood in this cold, sparse environment.

Hunting wild Arctic animals was the key to Inuit survival. The animals they pursued and caught included caribou, seals, walruses, beluga whales, polar bears, foxes, musk oxen, and a variety of fish and birds. In most cases, the Inuit made use of almost every part of the animal. For example, seals and caribou provided meat for food; skins for making clothing, blankets, tents, and boats; bones for making tools; intestines for making rain gear; and sinews that served as sewing thread. The Inuit made kayaks with sealskin or caribou skin over sturdy, lightweight wooden frames. They used sealskin or walrus skin to make umiaks, which they used for long trips and to hunt large sea animals.

Traditionally, the Inuit did not own land. Land belonged collectively to everyone and to no one in particular. Until the 1950s, the Inuit led a seminomadic life. They moved seasonally, establishing camps and following the migration patterns of the animals they

For centuries, the Inuit depended on their hunting skills for survival. A hunter uses a long-handled net to catch birds, *above,* and hunters haul a dead walrus up onto sea ice, *below.*

NORTH
POLE

ARCTIC OCEAN

GREENLAND

ARCTIC CIRCLE

Alaska
(U.S.)

• Grise Fiord

BAFFIN BAY

Tuktoyaktuk   Sachs
                    Harbor   Resolute •   Pond Inlet •
Aklavik •   • Arctic Bay   Clyde River •
        • Inuvik   BAFFIN ISLAND
Fort   • Holman   Broughton
McPherson   Paulatuk •   Cambridge   Spence   Island
                                    Bay   Bay   • Igloolik
                  • Coppermine   Gjoa   • Hall   • Pangnirtung
                                      Haven   Pelly   Beach
                        Bathurst   Bay
                        Inlet •
              NORTHWEST   Iqaluit •
              TERRITORIES   NUNAVUT   Coral   • Lake Harbor
                                            Harbor   • Cape   • Kangiqsujuak
                  • Yellowknife   • Baker Lake   Dorset   Quaqtaq •
                        Chesterfield Inlet •   Ivujivik •   • Kangirsuk   • Kangiqsualujjuaq
                        Whale Cove • • Rankin   Akulivik •   Salluit •   • Hopedale
                        Arviat •   Inlet   • Povungnituk   Nain •   • Makkovik
                                                                    Kuujjauq •   Postville •   • Rigolet
                                    HUDSON   Inukjuak •   North West   • Happy Valley-
                                    BAY   • Umiujaq   River   Goose Bay
                                          • Sanikiluaq
                      C A N A D A   • Kuujjuaraapik

U N I T E D   S T A T E S

Source: Department of Indian and Northern Affairs, Canada

An igloo can be a simple domed structure, or it can have a storeroom and passageway attached to the living quarters.

hunted. For transportation and hunting, the Inuit used dogsleds, kayaks, or umiaks. Living entirely off the land and surviving in a very harsh climate required great physical hardiness; superior hunting, fishing, and outdoor survival skills; and a supportive family and community life.

The Inuit lived in various types of houses, depending on the season and the materials available. In winter, they lived in igloos, dome-shaped houses made of blocks of ice, snow, or materials such as whale ribs or driftwood reinforced with snow. An experienced person could make an igloo in an hour or two. Celine Ningork, an Inuit from Pelly Bay, talked about living in an igloo. She said, "I don't even remember being cold or uncomfortable in one. When it got too old and you had to patch it up every day, you just went ahead and built a new one." During the summer, many Inuit lived in *haumuq*—tents made of animal skins. Soapstone oil lamps, called

During the summer, many Inuit lived in tents made of animal skins, *below*. The traditional turf house with an ice porch, *left,* is still used as a shelter by Inuit hunters.

kudlik, burned seal and whale blubber to heat and light the igloos and tents.

Because the Arctic is one of the most remote parts of the world, the Inuit have had very limited contact with people from other cultures for most of their history. Brief contacts occurred in the 1800s, when explorers and whalers went to the Arctic. Later, the fur trade brought more contact with outsiders, as did the exploration of the Arctic for natural resources. Yet because of the inhospitable climate and the long distances involved in traveling to the Arctic, few outsiders came—and most did not stay long.

In Canada, the Inuit way of life changed little until the 1950s. At that time, the fur trade began to decline, caribou became more difficult to find, and the traditional way of living from the land had become very difficult. The Canadian government decided to improve the conditions of Inuit life. The government persuaded many Inuit to leave their camps and move to permanent communities. There, officials provided permanent housing, schools, medical care, food, and supplies. These developments lessened the harshness of the Inuit way of life, but they also caused the young people to abandon some hunting and outdoor survival skills that were no longer needed. Although traditional skills and activities were no longer necessary, new opportu-

nities for employment were lacking. To combat this problem, the Canadian government helped Inuit establish commercial fishing and handicraft cooperatives.

Instead of living in igloos or tents, most Inuit families began to live in prefabricated houses with modern conveniences, such as heat, hot water, and electricity. The snowmobile has largely replaced the dogsled for winter

Since the 1950s, the Inuit way of life has changed dramatically. Snowmobiles have replaced dogsleds, rifles have replaced spears, bows, and arrows, and prefabricated buildings have replaced igloos, tents, and turf houses.

transport, as the motor boat replaced the kayak and umiak for summer transport. What was recently a nomadic hunting society that lived off the land is now a society living in permanent settlements with cable TV, fax machines, and supermarkets selling imported food. In 1993, the Canadian government signed an agreement to create the territory of Nunavut, the eastern part of the Northwest Territories, where Inuit are a majority.

While the Inuit lifestyle may more closely resemble that of other people in North America, the Inuit remain a distinct society with their own customs, beliefs, and legends that have been passed down through the centuries. One way to learn about Inuit traditions is to study their art. It could be said that art is a universal language. Although you may not be able to understand the words of a story told in Inuktitut, the Inuit language, you might gain an understanding of what the story is about by studying a drawing that illustrated the story. Art can be a window into a culture different from your own.

The Inuit often depict their history, folk-tales, legends, and religious customs in their art. This book examines the three major forms of Inuit art—sculpture, drawing, and printmaking. The art featured in this book comes from villages in the Canadian Arctic. Many of these communities have formed co-operatives to market and sell Inuit art to galleries around the world. All the art pictured in the following pages dates from the 1950s to the 1990s, the period of the greatest Inuit artistic activity.

Sculpture, Drawing, and Printmaking

Figure 1
Standing Caribou
Osuitok Ipeelee
Cape Dorset
1988

INUIT SCULPTURE—MOSTLY OF ANIMALS AND
people—has a lifelike vitality. Modern Inuit sculpture technique grew out of a much older practice of hand carving the tools, weapons, and utensils necessary for hunting, fishing, cooking, and shelter building. This basic survival skill was passed down from generation to generation.

Sculpture can be made out of many materials, including marble, bronze, wood, clay, concrete, iron, and steel. The Inuit usually use only materials found in the Arctic. These materials include a variety of local stones, as well as many animal substances such as whalebone, caribou antler, musk ox horn, and walrus tusk.

Standing Caribou **(figure 1)** by Osuitok Ipeelee is carved of stone and caribou antler. Like this piece, many Inuit sculptures are small enough to be held in one's hands.

Animals are a favorite subject in Inuit art. The Inuit people, who previously depended entirely on Arctic animals for survival, are keen observers of animals in the wild. This careful observation so important to hunters is also beneficial to sculptors. It helps them capture and re-create an animal's shape, gesture, pose, and expression in a work of sculpture.

Inuit sculptors portray many Arctic animals in their work. Polar bears, walruses, seals, musk oxen, caribou, geese, and other birds are all common subjects. When you look at Inuit sculpture, notice the sensitive way the artist portrays the strength and beauty of an animal.

The artist relates an attitude of respect and admiration in the majestic sculpture *Owl* (**figure 2**), which shows a proud-looking bird with widespread wings. A patterned texture was cut into the stone to represent feathers.

The Inuit frequently make sculptures of people also. Because Inuit sculptors typically use materials found in the Arctic and sculpt the animals and people common to that environment, their work shows a kind of intimacy with both materials and subject matter. The result is different from a sculptor who imports material from another continent and makes a statue of someone from a past century.

If you were going to make a sculpture out of a material in your environment and were to choose a subject closely familiar to you, what kind of sculpture might you make?

Figure 2
Owl
Artist Unknown
Inukjuak
circa 1955

Drawing and Printmaking

Modern Inuit printmaking and drawing began in the late 1950s with James Houston, a Canadian government worker. Houston, who was an artist himself, recognized the natural artistic talent of many Inuit. He encouraged drawing and introduced printmaking techniques to the people in Cape Dorset, one of the major Inuit settlements. (See map on page 11.) Houston hoped that Inuit artists might begin to sell prints and drawings as a way to supplement their income. This turned out to be a successful venture, and printmaking soon spread to other Inuit communities. Inuit drawings and prints are prized by U.S. and Canadian collectors. Alongside sculpture, the prints and drawings are sold in galleries and exhibited in museums.

Inuit mainly use colored pencils and felt markers to make drawings, but they use various techniques to make prints. Printmaking is almost always a collaborative effort. In a stone cut, an artist makes a drawing of the image to be produced. Then a stone cutter transfers the image to a stone block and carves out the stone surrounding the drawing's outlines. Finally, using a roller, a printer applies black or colored inks to the stone to transfer the image from the block to the paper. The printer makes a limited number of prints, usually 50 or 60. This process is called a print run. Then the stone block is destroyed so no other prints can be made.

Woman with Snowbird (**figure 3**) by artist Pitaloosie Saila is a beautiful and colorful combination stone cut and stencil of a woman holding a white bird. Half of the woman's face is colored red and the other half is colored blue. Saila did this because each side of a person's face is different. The artist said, "I designed it like a shadow, like one part of the face being in the dark. As if it wasn't brightly lit in the home in those days. Also, a face is different on both sides." About her art in general, Saila said, "The drawings I do are my heritage to my children, my grandchildren, and future generations. I draw what I have seen or heard; I draw about my life. I draw so the Inuit traditional way of life can be preserved on paper, and it is only when I draw that it will be shown."

The name of the artist who did the original drawing, as well as the names of the stonecutter and printer, might be cut into the design or be written at the bottom of the finished print. The names might be written in Inuit script, called syllabics, or they might appear in the form of a monogram. The date and title of the picture might also be written

Figure 3
Woman with Snow Bird
Pitaloosie Saila
Cape Dorset
1973

at the bottom of a print, as they are in Saila's work. A symbol signifying the community in which the print was made is also used. In this case, a red igloo appears under a row of syllabic letters. This igloo means the print was made in Cape Dorset.

Sculpture and Printmaking

Sculpture is a three-dimensional art form because it has height, width, and depth. However, prints and drawings, like paintings, are two-dimensional art forms. They have height and width but they have no depth. They are flat. In two-dimensional art forms it is easier to show many people and animals, and it is possible to show them in a surrounding landscape.

Sculpture has the advantage of being able to portray a figure from all sides—front, back, top, and bottom. A print, however, can show only one side of a figure. Usually sculptors do not color their works. They let the original color of the material serve as the color of the finished piece. Prints, drawings, and other two-dimensional forms of art are often made of many colors. Form and shape are generally more important in sculpture, while color and setting are more important in two-dimensional art.

Viewers can compare the subject matter of Inuit prints and sculpture, however. Both printmakers and sculptors frequently portray identifiable images of animals, family life, hunting, legends, and shamans—spiritual leaders believed to have supernatural powers, including the ability to communicate with the spirit world.

David Ruben Piqtoukun at work on a sculpture

Inuit art is usually classified as representational art. This means the artist creates a recognizable image—such as an animal. Until the 20th century, most painting and sculpture throughout history was representational. Some 20th-century art is abstract, or nonfigurative, rather than representational. Abstract art does not depict identifiable subject matter. Instead it may be a composition of color or shapes that do not directly suggest a subject. Abstract artists allow the means of image making—brushstrokes, color, shape—to overshadow or distort the subject matter. Often the question "What is this image?" cannot be answered for an abstract work of art, but it is easily answered for a representational work.

The Inuit do not have a word that means "art" in their language. They use the word *sananquaq,* which means "making a likeness." Making a likeness is a good way to describe Inuit art.

chapter three

Inuit Life Viewed through Prints and Sculpture

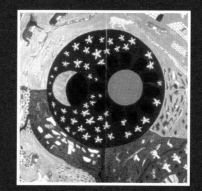

INUIT ART SOMETIMES DEPICTS THE ARTIST'S dreams. Many Inuit traditionally believed that dreams contained useful information for hunting and daily life. For example, they believed dreams could help them predict blizzards or locate animal herds.   The whimsical print *Dog Dreams of Seal* (**figure 4**) by Kingmeata Etidlooie shows a dog with a small seal in its stomach. Perhaps the dog is dreaming of its dinner.

As *Dog Dreams of Seal* tells the story of a dream, so does the following Inuit poem:

The Dream

Last night you were in a dream
I dreamed you were
walking on the shore
over the little stones
and I was walking with you
last night when I dreamed about you
I dreamed I followed you
I thought I was awake
I wanted you
as though you were a young seal
you were what I wanted
as a young seal
in the eyes of a hunter
before it dives because it's being followed
you were what I wanted
that's how
I wanted you
in my dream about you.

Figure 4
Dog Dreams of Seal
Kingmeata Etidlooie
Cape Dorset
1973

Dreams can provide lots of material for art. Can you think of some image or scene from a dream that you would like to put into a poem or a visual work of art?

Storytelling

The Inuit have a high regard for storytelling. Before missionaries introduced a writing system for the Inuit spoken language in the 19th century, storytelling was the primary method for passing down history and legends to younger generations. The storyteller often acted out scenes, made animal sounds and bird calls, or simulated rowing a kayak or running, as the story needed. A story might be told in a few minutes or over the course of several evenings. Storytelling was often like a theatrical performance, and a good storyteller was a cherished member of the community. Legends and stories are often told with many variations throughout the Arctic region.

The artist Davidialuk Ammitu Alasuaq was also a well-known storyteller. In his art, he often made images of the same stories he performed. In *Legend of Two Loons Opening a Blind Man's Eyes* (**figure 5**), Davidialuk illustrated the legend of a blind man who miraculously regained his sight when two loons submerged him in water. The man went on to live a long and prosperous life. In the print, two loons stand next to a man who is submerged upside down in the water. The print shows only the man's feet and part of his legs. Below the man's knees are short lines that represent ripples in the water. The two loons have rounded marks representing their feather patterns. The print has an irregularly shaped brown border. The border was made by leaving part of the stone around the design uncut. The artist then applied ink to this portion, which transferred to the paper as a border.

In Inuit myths and legends, animals often have special powers, such as the ability to change into human beings or the ability to speak. Sometimes these legendary animals captured Inuit people and brought them to live at the animal's den or nest.

One of the most important figures in Inuit mythology is Sedna, the sea goddess. Sedna is the caretaker of the marine life the Inuit depend upon—the whales, walruses, seals, and fish. Legends about Sedna are told in many versions throughout the Arctic. In one version, a bird disguised as a man tricked Sedna into becoming his wife. She lived with him for a time in a state of despair, in a remote place the bird had made their home. Eventually, she was able to escape with the help of her father and his boat.

Figure 5
Legend of Two Loons Opening a Blind Man's Eyes
Davidialuk Ammitu Alasuaq
Povungnituk
1973

But when the angry bird-husband discovered them, he created a violent sea storm. Sedna fell overboard. While she was clinging to the side of the boat, her father cut off her fingers so he would be able to escape. Sedna sank to the bottom of the ocean, and her fingers became sea animals—whales, seals, and fish. According to the legend, she lives on the ocean bottom as a goddess presiding over sea life. The Inuit respect Sedna and hope that she will provide a plentiful supply of sea life for them to hunt and fish. The goddess often appears in Inuit sculpture and prints.

Just as there are many versions of a single myth, sometimes a work of art has several different interpretations. One interpretation of the whalebone sculpture *Woman, Hand, and Bird Head* **(figure 6)** by Manasie Akpaliapik is based on the Sedna myth showing Sedna and her bird-husband before she fled with her father. The artist accentuates Sedna's hands, which are an integral aspect of the story. You can see the rough texture of the original whalebone in the figure of Sedna, but the

Figure 6
Woman, Hand, and Bird Head
Manasie Akpaliapik
Arctic Bay
1982

artist smoothed the whalebone when carving the bird. Manasie Akpaliapik took advantage of the different textures that can be achieved when carving whalebone.

The Sun and the Changing Seasons

The sun—and its absence in winter—plays an important role in Inuit life. In Inuit mythology the sun is personified as a woman—the way some people refer to the "man in the moon." *The Woman Who Lives in the Sun* (**figure 7**) by Kenojuak Ashevak and her husband, Johnniebo, has a bold design. It is done in a single color, as are many of the prints

from the early years of Inuit printmaking. Large rays emanate from the sun's face. The face shows a broad smile and features formed from simple shapes. The radiating lines on the chin represent tattoos. Until recently, some Inuit women tattooed geometric patterns on their faces as a form of body art.

In the Far North, there is much to rejoice about when the sun finally rises after the long, dark winter. The sun brings light and warmth. As the days gradually grow longer, snow melts, grasses and shrubs grow, and migrating animals arrive. *Nunavut* (**figure 8),** which means "our land" in the Inuit language, is another print by Kenojuak Ashevak.

Figure 7
The Woman Who Lives in the Sun
Kenojuak Ashevak and Johnniebo
Cape Dorset
1960

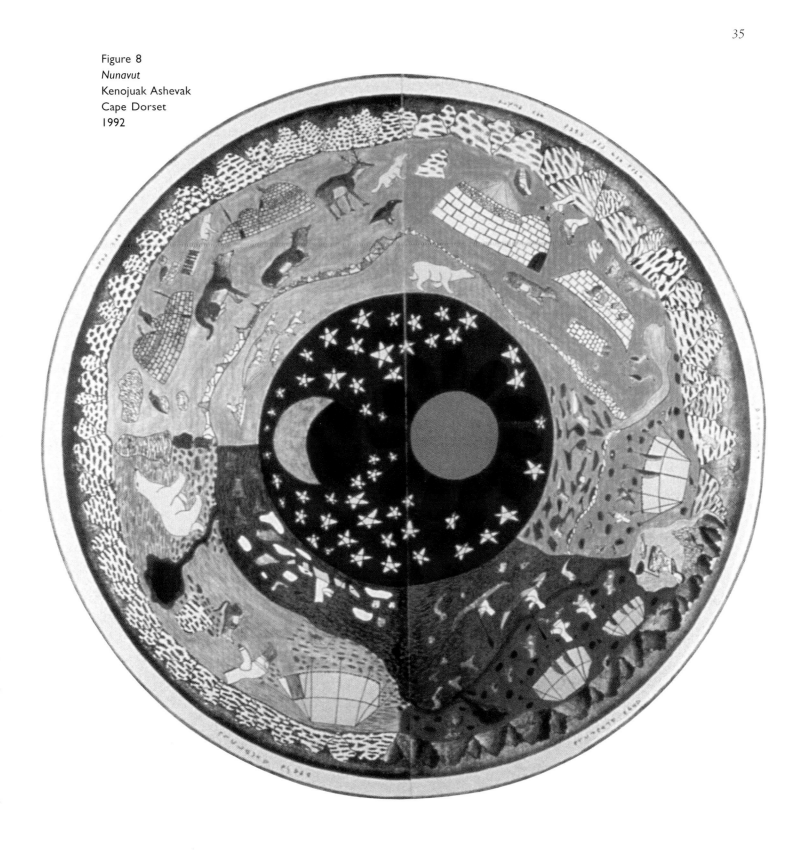

Figure 8
Nunavut
Kenojuak Ashevak
Cape Dorset
1992

Two details from *Nunavut*

This one, done in 1992, is complex in both design and color. The circular format contains four scenes, each representing a season.

The upper left portion represents a winter scene with groups of igloos, animals and birds, and a dogsled gliding over ice. The upper right portion shows spring. It looks similar to the winter scene, with human figures, igloos, and animals.

Changes begin to occur as we follow the design around clockwise. The ice begins to melt. In the lower right portion, summer has come, and the ice has melted. Tents have replaced igloos, and the people are hunting whales from kayaks. In autumn, in the lower left section, the ice is beginning to form again, as the temperature gradually drops and the days grow shorter.

This print shows how the land and the habitats and activities of the Inuit all change when the seasons change. You can see how the ground is covered with ice during much of the year. The Inuit syllabic inscription around the edge of the print reads (starting at the top): "Longer days in the year sliding with sealskin; Springtime; Summertime; In the fall during first snowfall; Middle of winter."

In *Masters of the Arctic*, an Inuit described how he felt about his land this way:

> Our land is like our soul. From the land we have gained all of our knowledge, our wisdom, our spirit, our past, our life.

The Arctic tundra in summer with melt streams, *left,* and in fall, *below*

We see only beauty, peace and a way of being when we are on our land. We call our land *Nunatsiaq*—the beautiful land. We change as our land changes.

Shamans

Many cultures around the world share a belief in shamans. In the Inuit language a shaman is an *angakoq*. As many Inuit convert to Christianity, shamanistic beliefs are becoming much less prevalent, but images of shamans continue to be a major theme in Inuit art.

A shaman's powers include diagnosing and curing sickness, predicting and controlling the weather, bringing animals into the range of hunters, finding lost objects, seeing into the past and future, and interceding with the spirits in other worlds—spirits who might be angry and cause suffering and death within the Inuit community.

The shaman was revered—but also feared—because of his or her powers. Usually a person could not just choose to become a shaman. A shaman had to demonstrate special traits, such as having prophetic dreams or miraculously recovering from a serious illness or injury. The person would then go through a harsh initiation process that might include long periods of fasting and exposure to cold. The aspiring shaman might also serve as an apprentice to an older, more experienced one.

In the belief system of shamanism, everything has a spirit that must be honored—and sometimes appeased. When hunting, for example, it is important not to anger an animal's spirit by violating the prescribed methods of killing animals.

Every shaman has a group of helping spirits. These spirits assist the shaman in his or her work. *A Shaman's Helping Spirits* (**figure 9**) by Jessie Oonark shows a shaman with his 12 animal-spirit helpers and one human-spirit helper. Helping spirits are attracted to the shaman because the spiritual leader has a bright light emanating from his or her body. This light cannot be seen by humans but can be seen by spirits. The shaman can use this bright light to see into the future and into faraway lands. A shaman might also use the light to find something, such as a hunter's lost harpoon.

Figure 9
A Shaman's Helping Spirits
Jessie Oonark
Baker Lake
1971

Figure 10
Bear Spirit Possessing Man's Soul
David Ruben Piqtoukun
Paulatuk
1982

Shamans also search for lost souls—souls that have been stolen or lost from a person's physical body. Death might occur if the soul is not located and returned to its human owner. The stone sculpture *Bear Spirit Possessing Man's Soul* **(figure 10)** by David Ruben Piqtoukun shows a tiny figure of a man inside the chest of a bear. The surface of the sculpture is extremely smooth, and color variations in the stone create an effect that resembles the color and texture of the bear's fur. The sculptor has portrayed the power and strength of the bear. In contrast, the soul is represented by a small human figure set into a cavity in the bear's chest. The task of the shaman would be to locate the lost soul, free it from the bear, and return it to its human owner.

A shaman is also believed to be able to change into the shapes of various animals, and many sculptures represent this phenomenon.

These works are called transformation pieces. In *Shaman Head* **(figure 11)** by Manasie Akpaliapik, the shaman is becoming some kind of fierce animal. Ears are sprouting, fur is growing, and sharp teeth are appearing. This is a shaman undergoing a transformation.

Sometimes shamans change into birds, so they can fly to distant places, such as the moon or the spirit world. On these trips, a shaman might influence weather spirits and animal-keeper spirits to look upon the shaman's community favorably. Shamans visit the sea goddess, Sedna, to plead with her if seal hunting or fishing conditions need to be improved.

A shaman also has the ability to become a skeleton. William Noah's print *Shaman* (**figure 12**) resembles an X-ray photo. The person's skin, flesh, and blood vessels have disappeared. All that remains are the skeleton and internal organs. Many Inuit also think that a shaman can become invisible. Becoming a skeleton was the first step toward becoming invisible.

The Hunt

One of the most defining characteristics of traditional Inuit life was the hunt. Inuit hunters used handmade spears and weapons to overpower the large animals they used for food and clothing. Without their expert ability to hunt and fish, Inuit could not have survived in the Arctic, where virtually no plants can grow. Although Inuit now buy most of their food at stores, some still do hunt. Rifles, however, have replaced spears, bows, and arrows.

Figure 11
Shaman Head
Manasie Akpaliapik
Arctic Bay
1989

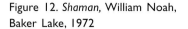

Figure 12. *Shaman,* William Noah, Baker Lake, 1972

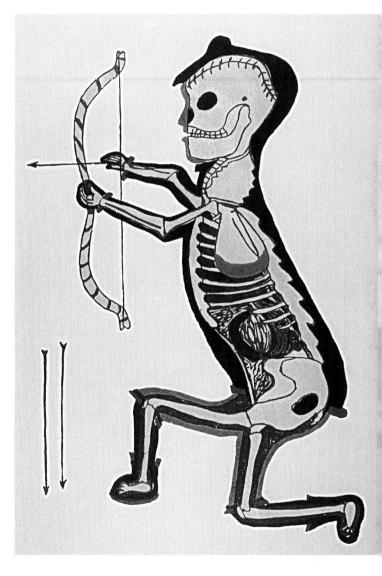

Figure 13
Joyfully I See Ten Caribou
Kananginak Pootoogook
Cape Dorset
1959

Kananginak Pootoogook was an expert hunter who made art when he was not tracking animals. His *Joyfully I See Ten Caribou* **(figure 13)** shows a hunter raising his hands to imitate the look of caribou antlers. This was a silent signal to his hunting party that he had spotted caribou.

Traditional hunting in the Arctic was often an endurance test and an athletic feat. Hunters sometimes waited hours at ice holes for seals to emerge for a breath of air. They also waited at riverbanks where caribou crossed during their migration. Caribou herds can be large, some-times containing thousands of animals. The sculpture *Archer* **(figure 14)** by Judas Ullulaq shows the anticipation of a hunter as he readies his bow and arrow. The following Inuit poem captures the spirit of the hunt:

> *A wonderful occupation*
> *Hunting caribou!*
> *But too rarely we*
> *Excel at it*
> *So that we stand*
> *Like a bright flame*
> *Over the plain.*

Figure 14
Archer
Judas Ullulaq
Gjoa Haven
no date

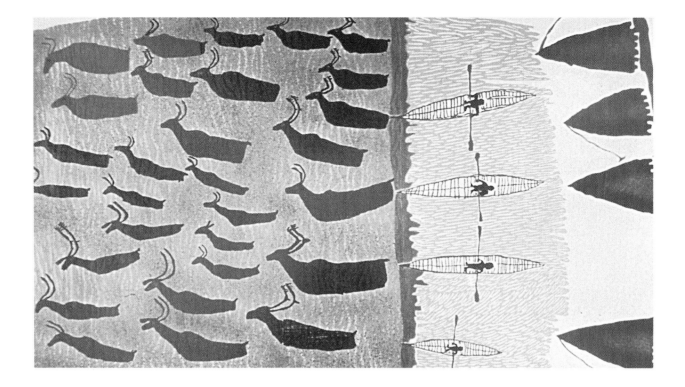

The print *Hunting Caribou from Kayaks* (**figure 15**) by Luke Anguhadluq shows a hunt in progress. A herd of caribou is swimming across the water to get to land on the other side. Four hunters in kayaks are pursuing the animals. On the right side of the print are four tents. The hunters have come to this site during the summer to camp and to hunt caribou.

Drum Dancing

Music, song, and dance are important to Inuit communities. Singing is often part of the everyday routine, and people write their own songs to sing. Dancing is a group activity often done to the beat of a drum accompanied by singers. Drums can be made out of a whale lung or caribou skin stretched over a bone or wooden frame.

Drum Dancer (**figure 16**) by David Ruben Piqtoukun is a beautiful stone sculpture of a figure playing a drum. The drum, shown as a round disk, is balanced on the ground by the drummer. Drum dancing is a tradition that almost died out but then experienced a revival in many Inuit communities. The artist, originally from Paulatuk but now living in Toronto, Ontario, in Canada, said this about drum dancing: "I have lived in the city too

Figure 15. *Hunting Caribou from Kayaks,*
Luke Anguhadluq, Baker Lake, 1976, *left*

Figure 16. *Drum Dancer,* David Ruben Piqtoukun,
Paulatuk, no date

long to dance." Although he is removed from the traditional way of life and activities of the Inuit, he uses the traditional life as inspiration for his art.

At community drum dances, the beat begins slowly and builds to a crescendo with the dancers moving along with the rhythm. Dancers sometimes imitate the movements of seals, polar bears, and caribou in their dances. The print *Drum Dancing* (**figure 17**) by Luke Anguhadluq shows a man beating a drum while energetically dancing to the beat. This vibrant print captures the joyous spirit of Inuit music and dance. An Inuit described the dance like this: "The drum pounds and so do our hearts as we sing and dance to share our souls."

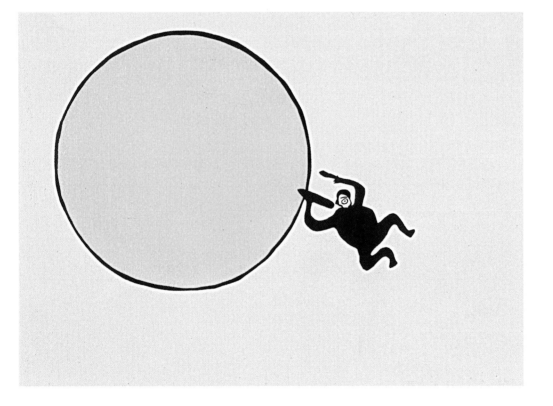

Figure 17
Drum Dancing
Luke Anguhadluq
Baker Lake
1975

Figure 18. *Aeroplane,* Pudlo Pudlat, Cape Dorset, 1976

Modern Life

A few artists have a great interest in modern technology and the changes in the Inuit lifestyle. Pudlo Pudlat's *Aeroplane* **(figure 18)** is a wonderful portrayal of an airplane flying above the Arctic landscape. Icy hills and seals rest below this colorful flying plane. Inuit fig- ures, dressed in traditional clothing, show a great interest in the plane. Two icebergs overlap the plane, one at the center, the other near the propeller, and one man seems to be standing on the highest iceberg to get a closer look at the plane.

Figure 19
New Forms in Our Path
Pudlo Pudlat
Cape Dorset
1986

New Forms in Our Path (**figure 19**), a print by the same artist, shows a musk ox and two birds approaching a series of four houses. The artist wants to show that animals have had to adjust to changes in the Arctic region just as humans have.

By looking at Inuit prints and sculptures, you can learn much about their art and way of life, the thoughts and ideas of individual artists, and the traditions and beliefs of the culture. Inuit life has been changing rapidly in recent years. The arrival of new technology has changed the Arctic hunting and fishing culture forever. The popularity of Inuit sculpture and prints has enabled older artists who formerly earned their living off the land to earn income by making art. This has encouraged many younger people to study and create art also.

While few people visit the Arctic region, meet the people, and see the land, you can learn about life in the Far North by looking at Inuit art. A woman named Ruby Angránaaq described making Inuit art—prints and drawings—in this way: "They are the messages we are sending out to the rest of the world."

These messages are dynamic images and beautiful works of art.

For Further Reading

Hancock, Lyn. *Nunavut*. Minneapolis: Lerner Publications Company, 1995.

Daitch, Richard W. *Northwest Territories*. Minneapolis: Lerner Publications Company, 1996.

Selected Bibliography

Brody, Hugh. *Living Arctic*. Vancouver/Toronto: Douglas and McIntyre, 1987.

Bruemmer, Fred. *Seasons of the Eskimo*. Greenwich, Connecticut: New York Graphic Society Ltd., 1971.

Canadian Eskimo Arts Council. *Inuit Sculpture*. Toronto: University of Toronto Press, 1971.

Masters of the Arctic. Ada, Michigan: Amway Corporation, 1989.

Roch, Ernst, ed. *Arts of the Eskimo:* Prints. Barre, Massachusetts: Barre Publishers, 1975.

Swinton, George. *Sculpture of the Eskimo*. Toronto: McClelland and Stewart, 1987.

Sources for Quotations and Poems:

The quotation on page 13 is from *Living Arctic* by Hugh Brody.

The quotation on page 22 is from *Inuit Women Artists* edited by Odette Lerous, Marion E. Jackson, and Minnie Aodla Freeman.

The poem on page 29 is from *I Breathe a New Song,* edited by Richard Lewis.

The quotations on pages 37–38 and 48 are from the *Masters of the Arctic* exhibition catalog.

The poem on page 44 is from *Seasons of the Eskimo* by Fred Bruemmer.

The quotation on page 50 is from *The Inuit Imagination* by Harold Seidelman.

The Artists

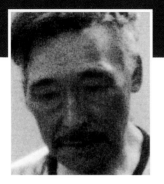

Osuitok Ipeelee,
Figure 1, *Standing Caribou,*
Cape Dorset, 1988,
Courtesy of Dorset Fine Arts

Pitaloosie Saila,
Figure 3, *Woman with Snow
Bird,* Cape Dorset, 1973,
Courtesy of Dorset Fine Arts

Kingmeata Etidlooie,
Figure 4, *Dog Dreams of Seal,*
Cape Dorset, 1973,
Courtesy of Dorset Fine Arts

Artist Unknown, Figure 2, *Owl,* Injukjuak, c. 1955, Courtesy of Canadian Museum of Civilization. Luke Anguhadluq,
Figure 15, *Hunting Caribou from Kayaks,* Baker Lake, 1976 and Figure 17, *Drum Dancing,* Baker Lake, 1975, Courtesy of
Public Trustee Office of the N.W.T., estate of Anguhadluq.

Davidialuk Ammitu Alasuaq,
Figure 5, *Legend of Two Loons
Opening a Blind Man's Eyes,*
Povungnituk, 1973,
Courtesy of La Fédération
des Coopératives du
Nouveau Québec

Manasie Akpaliapik,
Figure 6, *Woman, Hand, and
Bird Head,* Arctic Bay, 1982
and Figure 11, *Shaman Head,*
Arctic Bay, 1989,
Courtesy of Images Art
Gallery

Kenojuak Ashevak,
Figure 7, *The Woman Who
Lives in the Sun,*
Cape Dorset, 1960 and
Figure 8, *Nunavut,*
Cape Dorset, 1992,
Courtesy of Dorset Fine Arts

Jessie Oonark,
Figure 9, *A Shaman's Helping Spirits,*
Baker Lake, 1971,
Courtesy of Public Trustee
Office of the N.W.T.,
estate of Oonark

David Ruben Piqtoukun,
Figure 10, *Bear Spirit Possessing Man's Soul,* Paulatuk, 1982 and
Figure 16, *Drum Dancer* Paulatuk, no date,
Courtesy of Images Art Gallery

William Noah,
Figure 12, *Shaman,*
Baker Lake, 1972,
Courtesy of William Noah

Kananginak Pootoogook,
Figure 13, *Joyfully I See Ten Caribou,* Cape Dorset, 1959,
Courtesy of Dorset Fine Arts

Judas Ullulaq,
Figure 14, *Archer,*
Gjoa Haven, no date,
Courtesy of Judas Ullulaq and
Canadian Arctic Producers

Pudlo Pudlat,
Figure 18, *Aeroplane,*
Cape Dorset, 1976 and
Figure 19, *New Forms in Our Path,* Cape Dorset, 1986,
Courtesy of Dorset Fine Arts

Index

About the Author

Carol Finley studied art history at Northwestern University and did graduate work at Bryn Mawr College. She worked as a trader in the financial markets before pursuing a career in writing. She lives in London and New York City.

Photo Acknowledgments

© B & C Alexander, 8 (both), 10 (both), 12–13, 14 (left), 15 (all), 37 (both); Canadian Museum of Civilization, 14 (right); Indian and Northern Affairs Canada, 2, 5, 7, 23, 28, 31, 33, 34, 35, 36 (both), 39, 40, 43, 44, 45, 47, 48, 49, 50, 52 (top right and bottom right), (Art Gallery of Ontario, 18), (Leslie Boyd, 53 [top right]), (John Fowler, 52 [bottom left]), (Richard Garner, 20–21, 46), (Tessa MacIntosh, 52 [top center]), Patricia Wheeler Mayrs, 53 [top center]), Michael Mitchell, 53 [bottom right], (Michael Neill, 17, 32–33, 42), (John Paskievich, 52 [top left], 53 [bottom left and center]), (John Reeves, 52 [bottom center]), (Tom Skudra, 24–25, 53 [top left]).

Front and back covers, Indian and Northern Affairs Canada.

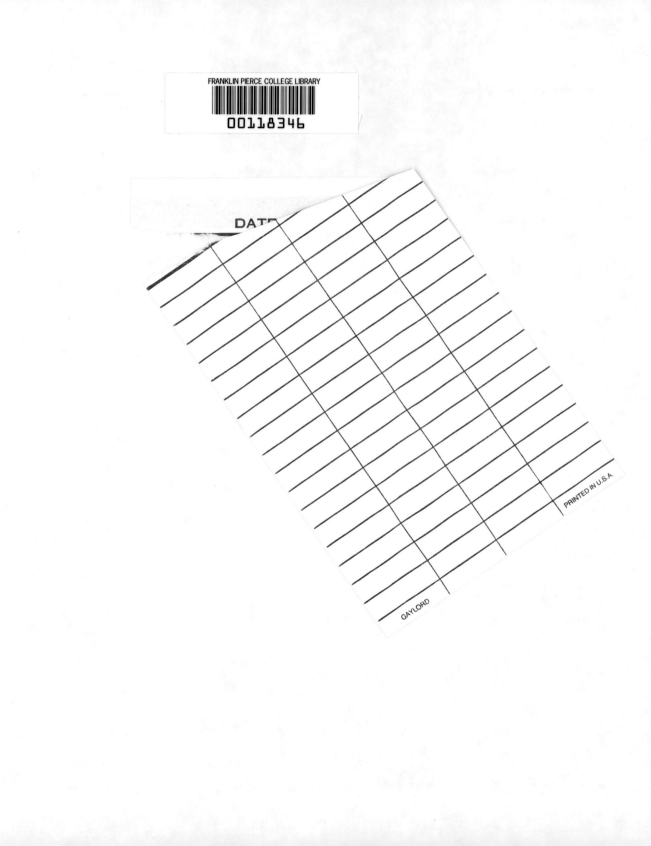

DATE

GAYLORD

PRINTED IN U.S.A.